IN PRISON

IN PRISON

PHOTOGRAPHS AND TEXT BY

DOUGLAS KENT HALL

HENRY HOLT AND COMPANY
NEW YORK

Published by Henry Holt and Company, Inc.,
115 West 18th Street, New York, New York 10011.
Published in Canada by Fitzhenry & Whiteside Limited,
195 Allstate Parkway, Markham, Ontario L3R 4T8.

Library of Congress Cataloging-in Publication Data
Hall, Douglas Kent.
In prison / photographs and text by Douglas Kent Hall.—1st ed.
   p. cm.
ISBN 0-8050-0592-7
1. Prisoners—New Mexico—Santa Fe—Attitudes—Case studies.
2. New Mexico State Penitentiary.   3. Crime and criminals—United
States—Attitudes—Case studies.   I. Title.
HV9481.S362N484 1988
365'.6'0978956—dc19   88-9237
                                    CIP

Henry Holt books are available at special discounts
for bulk purchases for sales promotions, premiums,
fund-raising, or educational use. Special editions
or book excerpts can also be created to specification.

   For details, contact:

   Special Sales Director
   Henry Holt and Company, Inc.
   115 West 18th Street
   New York, New York 10011

First Edition

Designed by Lucy Albanese
Printed in West Germany by H. Stürtz AG, Würzburg
10 9 8 7 6 5 4 3 2 1

Inside Prison Walls

LIFE SENTENCES
Rage and Survival Behind Bars
By Wilbert Rideau and Ron Wikberg
Times; 306 pages; $15 paperback

REVIEWED BY DANNIE MARTIN

Answers to questions people rarely ask about the prison experience and how convicts live in the shadow of their keepers are revealed in this bittersweet book about one modern dungeon and those who inhabit it.

What we learn in "Life Sentences" is universal — prisons are pretty much the same everywhere — yet there's a glaring difference between Angola prison in Louisiana and other maximum security facilities. In 1975, the warden of Angola appointed a lifer and aspiring writer named Wilbert Rideau to edit a prison publication called The Angolite.

The next warden, Paul C. Phelps, removed all censorship regulations and let Rideau publish anything as long as it was factual. Rideau became an objective journalist with a keen nose for research and soon, with the assistance of fellow prison writer Ron Wikberg, the walls of dark secrecy at Angola came tumbling down. The result is a unique collection of essays, stories and photos of "rage and survival behind bars," as the subtitle puts it.

"Leaving the bullpen, he strolled toward the cell area. Stepping into the darkened cell, he was swept into a whirlwind of violent movement that flung him hard against the wall, knocking the wind from him. A rough, calloused hand encircled his throat, the fingers digging painfully into his neck, cutting off the scream rushing to his lips. 'Holler, whore, and you die,' a hoarse voice warned, the threat emphasized by the knife point at his throat. He nodded weakly as a rag was stuffed in his mouth."

So begins an essay by Rideau called "The Sexual Jungle," A chilling and graph-

FROM 'LIFE SENTENCES'

Ron Wikberg, left, and Wilbert Rideau: editors of The Angolite, the Angola prison newspaper

ic depiction of homosexual rape followed by an account of the sexual mores of confined men. As do others, this piece leaves us with the sense that real people with feelings suffer such demented violence. These men are not caged thugs secured somewhere in the belly of society.

In recent years, as lengthy sentences and death penalties have become the norm, we hear the word "deterrent" used repeatedly by politicians and law enforcement bureaucrats. But in "Toward Realistic Justice," Rideau gives a prisoner's insight into the word. He points out that according to FBI statistics, police solve only 25 percent of all major crimes reported. A criminal therefore assumes he has a three-for-one chance of getting away. Not

a bad gamble. So how, he asks, can the threat of a long sentence deter a person who doesn't expect to be caught? The certainty of apprehension would be the deterrent itself.

The theme of justice gone astray is illustrated through harrowing accounts of real people. "The Escape of Nigger Joe" draws us intimately into the Orwellian world of justice by describing a man serving life on an extremely questionable murder charge. After serving 25 years, he ran away in despair. Though pardoned by the governor, he had to serve another 10 years because of lost good time on the escape charge.

Prison administrators have their say, from wardens to mainline guards. Regard-

ing long, non-paroleable sentences, we hear Phelps, Angola's current warden: "There's a need for hope. Talk to any prison administrator in the United States that's been on the job very long or knows anything at all about prisons, and if you ask him what is necessary to run a safe constitutional prison, hope is going to be the number one thing. Without hope, it's just a matter of sheer physical force."

The book contains a wealth of previously unpublished information about the basic operations of prisons, including the subtle interplay between convicts and guards, where in particular the unwritten codes, where guards purposely ignore rule-breaking to maintain a level of peace.

Several pieces rise above the degrading pathos of confinement and become downright entertaining. In "The Legend of Leadbelly," we learn of Huddie Ledbetter, a big, hardworking half-Cherokee who did hard time in Texas and at Angola. Known on the chain gang as "the number one man in the number one gang on the number one farm in the state," he was said to pick a thousand pounds of cotton in a day.

At night, he sang. He recorded his pardon petition in the cotton fields and sent it to the governor on tape: "If I had you Gov'nor O.K. Allen,/ Like you got me,/ I would wake up in de mornin'/ Let you out on reprieve..."

Leadbelly's talent saved him, and Ron Wikberg's journalism is now being practiced in the free world. But after 31 years at Angola, Rideau is still struggling for his freedom. As a black who killed a white at the age of 19, he fervently hangs on to his hope, and we are the beneficiaries. ∎

Dannie Martin, who has spent more than 25 years in jails and prisons, is co-author of the upcoming book, 'Committing Journalism' (W.W. Norton).

Between the Lines of Malcolm X's Life

MALCOLM
The Life of a Man Who Changed Black America
By Bruce Perry
Station Hill; 542 pages; $24.95

REVIEWED BY
GREGORY STEPHENS

People who love or hate Malcolm X often hold irreconcilable views — united only by the "X" that now serves as a million-dollar marketing symbol onto which our racial obsessions are projected. As Bruce Perry's ground-breaking biography, "Malcolm: The Life of a Man Who Changed Black America," makes clear, Malcolm was a complicated leader who spoke with Louise's mother appears to different languages to different audiences.

Perry, editor of "Malcolm X: The Last Speeches," has interviewed more than 400 people who knew Malcolm, including family, friends from Nebraska and Michigan, most of his family, fellow criminals in Boston and New York, prison officials and Black Muslim associates. The portrait that emerges "will comfort neither his detractors nor his idolaters," writes Perry.

Like many public figures, Malcolm fictionalized elements in his life to suit ideological aims. Perry says. His research suggests that the Malcolm Little we read about in the famous Alex Haley-edited autobiography is about as far from the "real" Malcolm as, say, Henry Miller is from the "Henry" in his autobiographical novels.

Perry disputes many of Malcolm's claims of racial victimization. "Despite his efforts to attribute his misfortunes to white racism, most of his interactions with whites seem to have been positive. Perry finds no evidence of a confrontation Malcolm said his mother, Louise, had with the Ku Klux Klan. Neither can he find evidence that the death of his father, Earl, who was run over by a streetcar in Lansing, had anything to do with a white hate-group called the Black Legion.

Malcolm also claimed that his half-white mother was conceived after her mother was raped by a white man in Grenada. After interviewing relatives in Grenada, Perry discovered that while Malcolm's maternal grandfather was a Scottish man, his relationship with Louise's mother appears to have been consensual.

Neither do Malcolm's tales of social workers splitting up his family have much basis, Perry says. Court records and friends indicate young Malcolm requested to be placed in a juvenile home because his mother was ignoring him. This may have been partly a result of her relationship with Earl, who family friends say was brutal to his wife and children. After Earl's death, Louise left her children to fend for themselves. But Malcolm later portrayed both of his parents in saintly terms, says Perry, growing enraged when reporters questioned him about his past.

One pivotal incident in his autobiography, when an eighth-grade English teacher told Malcolm that being a lawyer was "no realistic goal for a nigger," does seem to have happened, Perry says. Malcolm had flowered for a year in a juvenile home in Mason, share of racial confrontations, most of his interactions with

Perry says Malcolm engaged in homosexual behavior as a boy sporadic," he says.

Malcolm's attitude toward whites was also more complex

CHRONICLE FILE PHOTO

fair complexion and green eyes, Perry writes. Louise insisted her father had been a white "prince." She often scrubbed Malcolm fiercely. "I can make him look almost white if I bathe him enough," she told a neighbor.

While part of Malcolm's later denunciation of whites was a reaction to overt racism, another part seems to have been overcompensation for his own racial insecurity, Perry believes. "When we get into power we're going to kill all you yellow niggers!" he told a family friend who rejected his pitch for the Nation of Islam. He later said NOI had too many "niggers." He characterized the children of interracial unions as "racial freaks," for whom he felt pity.

Even when Malcolm dropped the "white devil" theory (that whites are inherently evil) after his pilgrimage to Mecca, Perry believes he still demonized whites when it suited him. He also continued to invent a person-al history of victimization, telling a reporter in Egypt that whites had killed his father and four uncles; that a white man had knifed to death one of his brothers before his eyes.

Some *Malcolm* followers will be offended by Perry's complex, warts-and-all interpretation, but the composite portrait is characterized by admiration and respect. "Malcolm's greatness was not his ego-boosting attempt to counteract white ethnocentrism with black ethnocentrism, but his enormous capacity for intellectual, moral, and political growth," writes Perry. No one who reads the book will ever be able to look

ducing homosexual activity was

whites was also more complex

This book is dedicated to all the convicts who freely gave their time and thoughts to help me better understand the problems of prison life. My hope is that my efforts in making these photographs and putting together the following text will help open the way for some new and more creative solutions to the prison dilemma in the United States.

We are living in the era of premeditation and the perfect crime. Our criminals are no longer helpless children who could plead love as their excuse. On the contrary, they are adults and they have a perfect alibi: philosophy, which can be used for any purpose—even for transforming murderers into judges. . . . Once crime was as solitary as a cry of protest; now it is as universal as science. Yesterday it was put on trial; today it determines the law.

—Albert Camus

O N E

What I remember most is fear. My first time inside, I felt as if my limbs were strung together with piano wire. Each sound cut to the core of my nerves. Sweat trickled down my back. My mouth tasted of steel. So intensely was my mind fixed on getting back to safety and breathing freedom that I had the disconcerting sensation I was seeing nothing, shooting nothing.

Hours later, I stepped through the gate a changed person. Each image I thought I'd missed unreeled in my mind just the way I'd caught it on film. They were chilling images of convicts existing as I thought men could never live. I began to assign new meanings to the words prison, justice, humanity, suffering, *and* fate.

I first went into San Quentin with Arnold Schwarzenegger. It was February 2, 1980. Early that morning, I left home for Albuquerque to catch the first flight to San Francisco. I had just swung onto Interstate 25 from Santa Fe when I saw clouds of black smoke stacked against the cold dawn sky east of the highway. Clusters of flashing red lights burned in a circle around the state prison. On the horizon, a helicopter, its strobe marker pulsing, dipped down from the Sandia Mountains to the south and skimmed the hills toward the scene. I assumed a fire had broken out at the prison.

I was right about the fire, but that was only part of the story. At the

Going to the Yard,
New Mexico State Prison,
Santa Fe

airport, people talked about a riot already three or four hours old. Hundreds of convicts had gone on a mad rampage. Hostages were being held. There was widespread destruction, brutality, and murder of both hostages and inmates—sketchy facts that made me uneasy about walking into San Quentin later that day.

San Quentin had its own problems. Three inmates had slipped away in the night. Security was tighter than usual. The guards were on their toes, doing their jobs with a cool and thorough precision.

What I recall most clearly about that morning is the sound of the outside gate closing behind me. The heavy steel grill crashed against the steel template and the lock shot home.

After signing a sworn statement that I was carrying in neither contraband nor weapons, I was frisked—which reduced everything to the lack of trust that set the tone for what I would find inside. The guard's practiced fingers slid quickly over my limbs, reading my body for drugs or concealed weapons, an act that caused the hair on the back of my neck to bristle.

We made our way toward the gym where Arnold and his friend and fellow bodybuilder Franco Colombu would meet the prison bodybuilders. Arnold moved with far greater caution than I'd ever seen him show before. More than once I caught him shooting a nervous glance back at a closing door, his uneasiness reflecting my own. Later, when he was surrounded by a crowd of the huge prison bodybuilders who were clambering to get a word of advice or approval, I noticed him moving to get his back against a wall or a fence.

We passed through a series of locked gates and doors. I began to notice that the light, mostly artificial or filtered, was at a premium, but later, when I printed my photographs, I was surprised to find that some of the cells were actually bright. I now realize that what I felt as I threaded my way into the heart of the prison had little to do with light; it was simply a gradual shutting down of the human spirit.

After all the publicity surrounding the 1980 riot in the Prison of New Mexico in Santa Fe, the tales of inhumanity and horror, the sensationalism and the sorrow, one expects the prison to loom up in some terrible, gothic way. But it does not. Instead, sprawled on a gentle slope that falls gradually westward toward the Interstate and the Rio Grande River, it looks forlorn and unworthy of its reputation—burnished some in the summer of 1987 by the daring escape of seven maximum security convicts.

The older buildings, rebuilt after the riot, though still scarred from fire and stained with blood, are squat, sand colored, and ordinary looking; with coils of concertina wire corkscrewing along the ground and ribbons of razor wire laced along the tops of the high mesh fencing, they have the appearance of some minor military installation—like the modest headquarters housing an obsolete warheads dump.

The new buildings, clustered together in two complexes, the North and South facilities, are simple, squarish structures decorated with bold graphics and accent colors that resemble a modern high school, an upbeat styling that fails to mask the fact that they are fortresses, relatively impervious to fire, whose primary objective is the maximum security detention of living human beings.

Franco Colombu and Arnold Schwarzenegger at San Quentin

Warden George Sullivan issued me an unrestricted pass into the Santa Fe prison. With it, I could go anyplace and have access to any prisoner who would consent to speak with me or allow me to photograph him. This cleared the way for the series of straightforward portraits I had wanted to shoot since my first morning in San Quentin. Those portraits constitute the core of this book.

Inside the Main Facility, I moved with complete freedom. I was authorized to go alone, but much of the time I passed through cell blocks, cafeteria, library, gym, classrooms, hospital, and out into the industrial shops with two convicts, Pedro Martinez and Brian Church. I was allowed the same freedom of movement in the new facilities, but because of the electronic security system it was easier to go with a guard.

After numerous visits to prisons, spanning a period of six or seven years, I can speculate about prison life; I can look at it and talk about it in the light of all I have seen and heard. I can even imagine what it would be

Arnold Schwarzenegger and Franco Colombu at Folsom

like to be there as a convict, although I haven't experienced it. This is the story of the convicts, the men and women who know first hand the feeling of being locked up and being at the mercy of a system no one—including those who control it—quite understands.

My own initial experience of walking into prison was colored by fear but pales when compared to the experience of a young convict being taken in for the first time. For Brian Iglesia it began in a car speeding toward a prison in Colorado.

"I was scared to death," Brian recalls. "I remember every detail of that drive. I kept looking over every little hill to get a glimpse of the prison. I felt that it would make it better if I could just see it—I mean far enough in advance to help calm me. So, I kept looking and looking. Finally, there it was and I froze. Then suddenly we were in a parking lot and I was really on pins and needles.

"There's this routine they put you through—checking you in, giving you

The Weight Yard,
San Quentin

clothes, making you take that shower and use all that crab lotion. And then you're thrown into the fish tank for two weeks.

"Right off the bat there's the pressure of having to prove yourself, to save your ass. On the streets it's okay to joke with somebody, but if you start that shit in a penitentiary you'll carry a label. If a guy jokes with you and calls you a punk, you better jump him right then and there or else it's going to be worse later on. You've got to make a decision whether you're going to end up being the one they push around all the time, considered a punk, or if you want to be known as a loner doing your own time—which is accepted if you let them know right off the bat. You don't have to be part of a gang or clique. You can be respected for being a loner, but you better be able to back up your shit because they're going to give you a hard time."

Eugene Mescal, a Navajo Indian, was sitting on his bunk, in a cell darkened by a threadbare blanket hung over the window, listening to a small radio. When I entered the cell he pushed the blanket aside, letting the dim north light slant onto the floor. He described his first day in prison as a confusing blur. "I'd heard all the stories," he said, "and I was always looking around, seeing who was behind me. Some other Indian brothers guided me, showed me the ropes. With that, I started doing my own time." He paused. "I'm surprised I have come all this many years and I'm still alive."

Another convict who'd spent more time behind bars summed up his feelings more philosophically: "Prison is a strange civilization," he said. "You crowd people from all different walks of life into one environment and expect them all to dress the same, eat the same, and live the same. It's a volatile situation. You deal with all kinds of emotions. You go through changes; you have to stand up for yourself, you have to prove things. On the streets, if you don't like the people hanging around one area you go to another. Here you can't do that. You size up the situation and work for your respect—however you can get it."

Respect, as he used it, was a key word. After a man had been stripped of everything else, except a few essentials, and then locked up, respect was the one thing he could still maintain in prison. Respect, I was told, defined the difference between convict and inmate. And to the prisoners, it was an important distinction.

Leonardo Baca

Leonardo Baca made it clear he considered himself a convict. The day I met him in Cell Block One he asked to be photographed holding a portrait of Pancho Villa that had been painted by his friend Fernando Ogas. For my photograph, Leonardo put on a straw hat and tugged the brim over his eyes. After I'd read the light meter and snapped the shutter, I asked how much he identified with that hero of the Mexican Revolution.

"In here, they've always categorized me as a radical," Leonardo smiled, drawing a comparison he obviously enjoyed. "They call me an activist because I try to do good for others. That's the way the system thinks about a convict. And there's a big difference between an inmate and a convict. *Inmate* is a modern word, a new title. He's a man with a number, someone the system manipulates, an individual who's into acting the way they want him to act. A convict—" he hesitated, choosing his words—"a convict is solid. He maintains his sincerity, his respect. He is righteous. The system cannot understand convicts because we are too strong. They fear our mentalities."

Susano Cardenas, Jr., nodded his agreement. "To put it simply, an inmate is a model prisoner. A con goes by the old rules. A con will look on from a distance, but an inmate will go over and stand next to the Man. A con stays behind the scenes, looking and seeing. A con is a whole lot wiser than an inmate—because he stands back and looks."

I'd found Cardenas in the law library, where he was mopping the floor. He paused and leaned on the handle of his mop. "I'm an old con," he said. "I know how to survive. And in these prisons only the strong survive. The weak ones don't make it. If you have a strong constitution you get through this shit. If you don't—" he shrugged. Then his jaw hardened: "Me—I'd sooner die than back down."

To make his point, Cardenas dug from his shirt pocket a vial of the nitroglycerine tablets he took for his bad heart. "I could drop dead any minute," he said, his eyes narrowing. "So I don't give a goddamn. That's the old tradition. Either you stand up for yourself or you don't make it in here.

"Everyone has a different approach and a different way of thinking. In the old school, you never talk to the Man, you never stand near the Man. You've got the con, then the inmate, and at the bottom of the line: the rats. Rats, snitches, or punks, they're the lowest, down with the cowards, the filth. There are people who try to intimidate and win respect by loud words. But it don't work. They're the kind of people who have their balls stuck in their throats. Not where they should be." He grabbed the crotch of his pants and gave a hard tug. Amen.

For Rocky Shifflett winning respect didn't mean throwing up a barricade and standing alone; there were some finer points to consider. Rocky had a flag of thick gray hair and a full beard, which gave him the appearance of a wilderness prophet. He fixed me with cool blue eyes and his statements came sure and quick. He had thought the words through carefully and he repeated key phrases he wanted to sink in. "There are guys in here who are bad—bad dudes. Okay, so it's true. In a penitentiary setting, I'm considered a bad dude. I haven't done seventeen years in thirteen different prisons because I'm a nice guy. When push comes to shove, I'll hurt you before I'll have you hurt me. If I have to stay in this pen, I'm going to stay in it healthy. So if I even suspect that you're going to do something to me, I'm going to do it to you first and worry about the consequences later. Okay, so I'm a bad dude, but I know this is where I have to live. You cannot alienate yourself from everyone. Which means that as bad as you are, you've still got to have friends. Because nobody can stand alone."

TWO

One night I had this dream about the doors. I went around with a welding torch and burned the fuckers open and then I welded them like that—open. I went out to the warden's office and wrapped the welding cables around his throat and tightened them until that motherfucker's eyes popped out so far they seemed as big as his bald head. I woke up and nothing had changed. I was depressed all day long.

—Anonymous

Alejandro Garcia is a legend in the pen. He claimed that his years of being inside had made him mellow, but I couldn't see it. If he had pulled back from politics into the carapace of his art, it was only temporary. His anger was still there. The fires were banked for the present but they burned deep. I felt the sting in his words. When he spoke, it was as if he were peeling away his own skin and flesh in layers and baring the bundle of raw nerves that throbbed on the inside.

"I don't believe in penitentiaries," he declared. "And I hate this one," he spat. "I've been here for so damn long, you know. I'm on my fifteenth year. Sure, I do my trips here. I do my paintings and write my poems. It seems that after fifteen years I'd give up, I'd just say—man, to hell with it. But it doesn't work like that inside of me. Because ever since I was young I've seen the struggle. I've seen the political doubt and the corruption and all that bull that put us where we are.

"I find myself in bad situations in this penitentiary, chains that can't be broken. They can't find any way to keep us together without us becoming radical. So the institution turns us against each other to keep control. If they don't have control, they get all afraid their system's going to go to hell.

"There's a few of us that've tried to break the chain, but it's hard because our word doesn't go out. I've been politically active and all that bullshit. I saw what needed to be done and started thinking there is only

Alejandro Garcia

one way to do it, because we're not given an out. We're not given a voice. The only time we find one is through violence." The last word ended in a hiss. Silence.

"People like me," he continued, relaxing a little, "we're going to be political all our lives. But I gave up a lot of the struggle to mellow down. I let them pass it on to somebody else, because I'm getting old in here. I came in as a teenybopper and I find myself growing gray hair. I look in the mirror and say: 'Hey, man, you can't wear suspenders no more. It's past that time.' And I hate it, I hate the situation because I see what I'm turning into. I'm good in heart but those people, they get you in corners.

"People say: 'These guys in prison aren't worth a damn.' But we're good people. I mean, good in heart. We love, we care. Sure, there's always going to be the psychotic that runs around killing kids and all that shit. But, hey, they've got to come and deal with our laws inside the prison. We have our governments in here. We take care of those fuckers."

Convicts settled their scores with laws that often demanded violent ends—an eye for an eye, and worse. I had witnessed it in San Quentin. Stepping out into the yard, bright from the hard winter sun, I'd seen a group of convicts suddenly close around one man, heard him cry out, and then watched the group disperse, leaving the man in a heap on the concrete. It was like a dance in a dream, over in an instant. "Justice," muttered a convict standing near me, "does get done." The alarm sounded and a stretcher crew arrived.

"Sure, we're from the other side of the tracks," Alejandro continued, his eyes burning, "but that don't mean we're idiots. You know, we may not be literate in the English language. We're Mexicans. And to deprive us of our own race and our own language is their way of trying to keep us down in the muck.

"We're people from a race that's beautiful," he cried. Turning, he searched through a stack of small paintings. He pulled a portrait out; it was of a young Mexican as a god—reality and mythic symbolism masterfully blended in a fierce Mexican tableau. "Check the guy out. It's the struggle of

The Kitchen,
Main Facility,
Sante Fe

what we are, what we've been. For what? To end up in prison cells. Shit! We come from a race of kings, man, we come from a race that had goodness, knowledge. All our theories were based on love."

Anger welled up in his voice. "We're people, man, we're not creatures. We just grew up doing what other people forced us to do. And now we're in here like a bunch of dogs. Well, I don't want to be a dog. It's going to take years to get away from the prison influence, from having a government slap you around and say you're supposed to be humble, meek. 'Let me slap you on the other cheek,' they say. 'That's our philosophy, and if you don't live by it, God's going to punish you.'

"I'm not the dirty dog these people make me out to be. My growing up was difficult because my folks were under the thumb of a government they thought was out to help them. But they couldn't make it. It's hard when you've got kids that you love and want to feed. So we find our solutions. We say, fuck it, I'm going to make a buck whatever damn way I can."

He forced his words through clenched teeth. "I saw this turn to shit—so I found my own answers. I said to myself: 'You're not wrong in beating that son of a bitch up and taking his bucks. You know how he earned it—the same way you're getting it.' " He sighed, but the edge remained in his voice. "I'm not trying to say crime is right. I'm asking which crime? What about the little girl who's being pimped around and fed to the people that've got the bucks. That's wrong, that's morally wrong. We know that. It's sinful for the guy to go out there and say give me ten bucks and take my little sister. But who is more the criminal—him that's having to pimp her because he wants to live and help her to live or the punk that's trying to buy her, the punk with the money?

"Those people out there who are running all the games on the street, the people with the bucks and the power, they're saying: 'Let's kill those convicts on Death Row. I mean, we're Christians, man, but, hey, those guys on Death Row got to go.' They call it justice. Well, they're turning into the same damn animals they're bitchin' about us being."

He was silent until it became uncomfortable. "People out in the streets right now don't have time to smell roses and shit. They're in the rat race. In here we've got time. That's all we got, man. And we long for it. When something comes through, you know, it's glorious. It's new. But almost nothing comes. I can't smell shit through there." With the heel of his fist, he struck the narrow glass that allowed him to see little more than a vertical

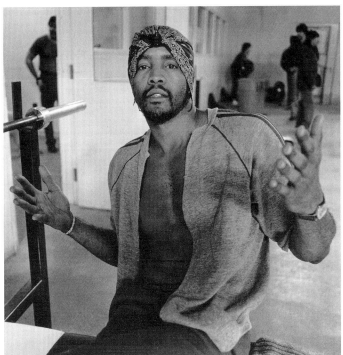

Convicts, Main Facility, Santa Fe (left)

The Gym, North Facility, Santa Fe (right)

strip of the concrete wall of the next building. "I can't even open it. So what do I got to live in?—a cell that's all cramped up. I'm a person whose instinct is to produce, you know. Look at me. I can't move. Sure, I need help, I need people to come in and check me out and say: 'Hey, man, you're not the dirty dog everyone says. You did what you had to do.' Yeah, well, survival is all I got. But that's life.

"Maybe you hear me talk like that and think I'm antireligious—but I'm not. I've got my own god. And it's not the guy they portray sitting out there on the throne, the guy without a face, you know, the guy shining like a dog. I can't go for that shit. I can't go for the so-called Christians because they're the ones that got me in here.

"If there's any kind of message that needs to get out to the people right now—especially to our races, especially the dogs that are down here, and I don't mean just the Mexicans or the black dudes, I mean the ones the government considers white trash—the message is this: We don't belong here. But we don't have all those big bucks that let us go around saying, 'Well, I don't give a fuck if I take your job or take away that little banana stand you've got there. I'm out for me. I run this place. I make the law. And if you don't follow that law then you're against me. And if you're against me then I'm taking you out.' That's the theme, man, that's the whole story behind it all. That's why I'm in here, and it pisses me off!"

THREE

I'm in this time for murder. The dude needed killing real bad.
I still remember just how it felt to put the knife in. Easy.

—*Anonymous*

A surprising number of convicts were proud of their records. A few said they'd seen the light and wanted to go straight, but many more confessed that they would return to crime. Some were defiant: the system could go fuck itself; others admitted that crime was the only skill they had, something prison had done little to change.

The reasons for becoming career criminals varied with the individual, ranging from necessity to boredom. Brian Iglesia went into crime as a blatant act of protest and revenge that grew out of the bitter disillusionment he suffered after duty in Vietnam. "For two years after Vietnam I was on the run with this team, pulling off commercial burglaries. We never got caught—and I'm talking about several hundred break-ins. Anything that had a government sticker on its doors we broke into. That's how much we hated this government. We went on a two-year rampage. The last job we pulled was in 1969, which is past the statute of limitations—so I can talk.

"We made headlines. There were three other guys and me. We had two women. We used two vans, two Mustangs, walkie-talkies, the whole thing. Two television shows that helped us put it together were *Mission Impossible* and *It Takes a Thief*. They gave us the idea for the walkie-talkies and the idea for having the girls out in front of the place we were knocking off. They'd have a flat on one of the Mustangs, get the car jacked up, and then report on the condition of the street into a walkie-talkie hidden in the trunk. That stuff doesn't just work in Hollywood."

Vietnam made Brian turn to crime, but it also limited the kind of crime he would do. "I've never committed an act of violence since I came back from Nam. Maybe it sounds strange to you other people, but we convicts do have morals. We're not just animals. There are certain things we will not do. I don't do armed robbery. I have always been scared that I would have to pull the trigger. I don't do house burglary for several reasons. Number one: you worked hard for what you've got. Number two: you could walk in on me and then I've got an eyewitness. So in order to save my ass I've got to do away with you. And I don't want to do that."

Philip Cordova, a slight, soft-spoken young man, serving a long sentence for his last conviction, admitted bluntly that he was a robber. In the same frank manner he took the opposite view of violent crime. To him, armed robbery was a narcotic. It had little to do with pulling the trigger or causing him any immediate concern about the violent consequences of his act.

"There's a thing I feel about armed robbery," he said, "it's addictive. You walk in a store and you take control of all the people in it. No matter if it's one person or twenty, you have that sense of control. You get a high off it. And the money is easy.

"I don't do burglaries because you've got to go out and sell all the stuff. Robbery is cash money. You can make an easy thousand bucks for a minute's work. It's simple, the money's good, and it's quick. But the time is big. This time I'm doing ten to fifty years. I've seen five parole boards and been denied in all of them. Whenever they decide to parole me I'll parole to twenty-nine years flat. So I have a stretch to go." His smile grew thin. "I'll probably get out pretty old."

Ron Brown wastes little time thinking about getting out. As he put it on the winter afternoon we talked in his cell: "I'm doing a natural life. I've only got one discharge and that's death."

Prison has been a part of Ron's thinking since childhood. "When I was just a little kid I remember dreaming about being in prison. And in my dreams it wasn't that bad," he paused, smiling. "It wasn't something that could scare me. Prison was just something to try not to get into.

"I came from a middle-class family and I'm the only one out of the seven kids that ever got in trouble. I was a throwback from someplace. I think that happens a lot more than people want to talk about. People always like to make excuses about why they do things. I just don't happen to have an excuse. I really don't believe I've ever done anything wrong.

"I fell the first time when I was nineteen. That's when I went to the joint. I had been busted before. But I was just a youngster doing wild youngster stuff, stealing cars and shit. My daddy paid the bills until I was nineteen. Then I had to start paying.

"I slid right in from the bottom. My first bust was for breaking and entering. I was in the army and when I got out of jail I deserted. They were playing games with me anyway. So I had to do a year-and-a-half army time. I got out of that and they busted me for car theft. I did thirteen flat in Iowa—my first step into the big time.

"While I was in jail I decided I didn't want to be there so I took out a sheriff—and I damn near got away with it. Damn near—" He smiled.

"I picked up fifteen more years for that and after I hit the joint I picked up six more numbers inside the walls. Sixty years is what I ended up with and I did thirteen flat before I discharged it.

"I was out for seven years. I did anything I wanted. I figured after I'd done so much time, why change it? I never really went big time. That's not my style. But I took whatever I wanted. I never cared what the laws read—I didn't write them. I stuck to my laws. My laws are stricter than their laws."

Ron's laws were very specific: "Under no circumstances never snitch. You die first. Never do anything unhonorable, anything that will put you in the category of weakling, snitch, pussy, or punk."

"How do you define a punk?"

"A punk is somebody who gives up pussy—under force. If he's a homo on the streets and comes in here and gets laid, that's his business. But if he's not gay and somebody in here threatens him and he gives it up, then he's a punk. But there's very little of that here, which is surprising for a joint. I'm a transfer from Iowa State and in that pen them girls hit the yard like big time, wearing dresses and makeup, the works. They had a lot of punks there and everybody played that shit. If you had an old lady it's nothing. You just had an old lady, that's all. I thought this kind of place would run into that real heavy but it's not. There's a stigma against it. Maybe it's the Mexican culture that dominates the place. To them it is unmanly to fuck punk. But that's their own problem. To me, the main thing is to maintain your manhood with honor."

Ron Brown

*Press Operator, Prison
Industries, Santa Fe
(left)*

*Convict, Main Facility,
Santa Fe (right)*

"Would you say that you function better inside the prison than outside?"

"I don't like to say that but I'm realistic enough to know it's the truth. On the bricks, I always have problems with my social behavior. If I don't like what somebody says I do something about it. Out there you can't do that. In here, it's the thing to do. If they hassle you, you do something about it. And if you don't, then that's where you're in the wrong.

"Prison life fits my rules perfectly. I am a convict and I have never done an unhonorable thing. When I was a youngster coming into prison, I made my rules. I knew what I would do. I have done some hurting things to myself but it has always been in an honorable situation. A lot of people said: you're choosing the wrong road. But in the long run it was the right road for me."

So there were career criminals and career convicts. The latter had been created by the system, hardened and turned bitter. On one of my last trips inside, I asked a convict what he would do if he could go back to the streets.

"There's no way," he said. "But if I could leave today, man, I know three people I'd kill—just bigger than shit," he said. "And if they didn't catch me I'd keep doing what I wanted until they did catch me." He barely smiled. "Prison's not that tough."

Stanley Ray Dennis dealt drugs. "Shorty," as he is called by fellow convicts, has a baby face with fine sandy hair and a light sprinkling of freckles. He was raised on one of the larger ranches in eastern New Mexico, but he never became a part of that life. Maybe it was the hard work, the long hours, or just the isolation; whatever, he threw it over and went into trafficking.

"In 1968 when I joined the Marine Corps I started using drugs—down on Hollywood Boulevard in L.A. I was doing a three-year hitch but after twenty-two months they said I was unable to adapt to military service and I got a dishonorable discharge. I think it was because I got off into the peace movement on Hollywood Boulevard. I had orders to go to Vietnam three times and three times I went AWOL. Twice the FBI busted me in Albuquerque. The third time, I did eight months in the Camp Pendleton brig and they kicked me out.

"I went to Laguna Beach, California, bought sixty pounds of pot, and took it back to Tucumcari. I started dealing drugs and I've dealt drugs ever since."

"Why did you choose to deal? It wasn't the lack of opportunity."

"No. I just like the life-style. I make a lot and I spend a lot. I have a good time. I party. I do drugs."

"So when you get out you don't think twice about picking up right where you left off?"

"That's right. The first time I came to the penitentiary was in 1971. I got two to five years for selling hash. I did four years and four months on it. I was out three months when I got busted with a gun collection I was going to trade for drugs. I got a two-and-a-half to ten-year habitual sentence. I finaled that in 1982, stayed out three and a half years and then got busted for twenty-two counts of forgery and one count of conspiracy. Now I'm doing six three-year sentences, all of them running wild. That means they're stacked one on top of another—eighteen years total."

"Isn't that enough to convince you to go straight?"

"I doubt it. My connections on the outside are the kind where I can go and get as much drugs as I want. If I want a half-pound of speed I can go get a half-pound of speed or whatever amount of whatever drug I want. They'll let me have it because they know I am good for the money, that I will pay them before I come back for more. I've been in the drug scene now for

Guard, Santa Fe

twenty years. I really don't know anything else. When I hit the streets in 1982, I got married. It lasted about a year and three months and during that time I was doing drugs and my wife never knew it. When she did find out about it, that's when she left me. After she left I started picking up big quantities of drugs and a year later I got busted.

"I don't do violent crimes. To rob a store or threaten your life with a gun," he shook his head, "I couldn't go do that. But to go get a half a pound of speed and sell it to you, I could do that. I don't like to put people in jeopardy. I just like to have a lot of money. If I see something I want, I want to be able to buy it right then. I don't want to wait until the end of the week to get my paycheck to buy it."

"So there's no way you're going to change, right?"

"Out of the last fifteen years I've been in the joint almost twelve years.

I've got this eighteen-year sentence to do and I've only got a year done on it, so I figure I'll probably do anywhere from eleven to twelve years on it. When I get out I'll be almost fifty years old and what are you going to do when you're fifty years old and coming out of this place? You're already too old for a hard job so I'll probably just go back to selling drugs."

I ask how his family took his being in prison. Shorty crossed his cell to a shelf and took down a folder containing photographs of his children.

"I've got three daughters," he smiled, holding the photographs so I could see the kids. "One of them I've never seen. Two of them I'm real close to. I love my kids. My oldest daughter understands me. To her, I'm an outlaw. That's what she calls me. She accepts that. She's been coming to see me since she was four years old. She's seventeen, so I've actually lived with her only about four years of her life. But that don't mean she don't love me. She loves me; she tells me she loves me.

"What can I say?" He opened both hands. "I was born a hundred years too late. A hundred years ago I could have lived the life-style I want to live—like the Jameses, Sundance, whatever.

"My kids accept me the way I am. I've got a daughter who'll be two next month. My wife don't come to see me, but she lets my sister bring the baby to see me. She'll be probably ten or eleven years old when I get out of the joint. I hope she accepts me like my oldest daughter does. I've never lied to my oldest daughter. A lot of people come to the joint and their wives tell their kids that dad is working or something. My daughter's always known I was in the joint. When she was four years old she would come and say I know what this is, this is the joint. She's a real sweet kid. She's never been in trouble and I hope she never will be. She doesn't do drugs. She just tells me: 'I've seen what they do to you, I don't need to try them. It's your life, you just live it like you want to. I'll always be here to see you. You'll always be my dad.' "

FOUR

Four years inside the walls is like getting a degree from Harvard or someplace. You can't find no better teachers.

—Clarence Martin

Like most prisons, this one's counterproductive," Steve Bishop said, putting down the dog-eared paperback he'd been reading during the time he was free to walk the corridor outside his cell. He reached out and laced his fingers into the mesh wire fencing that separated the upper tier of cells from those on the lower level: "Instead of encouraging young guys to get educated and learn some type of trade so the return rate isn't so high," Bishop said, "they don't do anything. When you put a guy in a cage like this for twenty-four hours a day and you let him out ten minutes a day to take a shower and a few minutes more to stretch his legs and maybe push a little iron, then you're offering him nothing that's going to change him. So when you put that guy back out on the street he's the same man he was when he came in here—except he's probably a little sharper con-wise."

Prison produces a certain mindset. Not only are the prisoners confined physically, they are also locked up mentally. The penitentiary is a small civilization initially organized around the idea of punishment. That has remained its immediate concern and anything beyond that idea seems to be more an afterthought than a concrete plan to bring about positive change.

Convicts are complicated individuals whose lives are only further compounded by being confined to a cell. Different people confessed that the experience made them crazy. I heard this outcry repeatedly. "You're a rat in a cage. They back you into a corner. You get desperate and you're at the

Convicts, Main Facility

mercy of other men's desperation. You start looking for anything that will help you keep your sanity. You try to blend into the society. You pull together."

This creates gangs; it produces professionals. If these people were crooks before, they become criminals in the pen. And prison as a potential tool of reform and rehabilitation is largely defeated. One reason is that basically the treatment never varies from the day a person is locked up to the day he or she is allowed to walk out. So they look for options.

"The sky's the limit to what you can learn in the joint—good or bad," Brian Iglesia said. Iglesia was editor of the *New Mexico Prison News*, which has offices in the southeast wing of the Main Facility with the prison education department. He had given me a tour, pointing out the hate wall, where magazine staffers collected stories of special concern to prisoners. The current display dealt with a rapist on trial in Albuquerque. A convict

Weight Room, North Facility (left)

Recreation Area, North Facility, Santa Fe (right)

stopped pecking at an electronic typewriter to ask about the spelling of *cancel*.

Iglesia called out the letters then rocked back in his chair. "You can become anything you want in here—author, artist, whatever—because you've got time to devote to it. On the street, you've got to go to work, mow the lawn, all that stuff that goes along with being in the rat race. The bottom line is if you've got time for learning something respectable you can also dedicate more time to becoming a better criminal—depending on how your mind works and what's available to you. You can rehash the mistakes you made that put you in here, talk to the old ones who committed the same crimes, and hone it down to the perfect crime. Then when you get out you can give it another shot."

Bishop claimed to be a case in point. "When I first went to prison," he said, "it was for drug use. I didn't know anything compared to what I know now. All the real crimes I committed on the street were from things I learned in prison. When I left that federal pen the first time, I had a schematic of every safe being used for bank nightdrops and stuff like that. I had a complete file. I was twenty-four years old. When I went in, I wouldn't have known how to open a safe if I'd had the combination. Instead of having people put me to work or make me go to school or try to teach me a trade, they just sent me to a maximum security prison for seven years and left me there to do my time."

Pedro Martinez knew the futility of finally being free but trapped by ignorance and a record. "I have been in prisons and reform schools since I was a little kid. The first time I came into PNM I was eighteen. I came in for possession of a joint. I got two to ten years—for possession of one joint. I did two years flat on that sentence, then I went back to court and got eight years suspended."

We had just visited the prison industries buildings, where convicts cut and sewed prison clothing, stamped license plates, and made wood and metal furniture. They worked on what they claimed was mostly outdated equipment, preparing themselves for little more than frustration when they went outside to look for work. That story was all too familiar to Pedro.

"I tried to work when I hit the street but I didn't have any skills and all I had was the twenty-five dollars they gave me when I left. I even applied for a job picking up garbage for the city. And when I filled out the part of the form where it asked if I'd been convicted, I said yes and gave the reason. And that was the reason for my not getting the job.

"Then I went to the employment office. The only thing the interviewer had to suggest was vocational school. I knew he was right, but I had to have something to live off of, something to sustain me while I went. The only thing the schools were offering was the training. I didn't know grants ex-

Jerry Snyder, Artist, Main Facility

isted. Now, they make an effort in here to tell you about these opportunities, but not in the past.

"I ended up going back to Mexico and bringing in drugs. Then one day I got a phone call that my little girl had been run over by a car so I went to the hospital. I spent a lot of time at the hospital, staying overnight and stuff. But the drug business doesn't slow down for anyone's problems and my schedule got all mixed up because of what had happened to my daughter. I was in a rush. I had people waiting on drugs. And I was trying to do too much. I left for Mexico to score a load of heroin and I was hurrying to get back to the hospital, taking chances I never would have taken, when I got busted by the customs people at the border."

The guard at the station separating prison industries from the cell blocks stopped us. He frisked Pedro, checked my camera bag, and then waved us through. We paused to watch two convicts working out on a speed bag.

"I spent about six months in jail," Pedro went on. "I tried to think of anything that would give me a way to stay out there. I finally decided to try preaching the gospel. And I was sincere about preaching the gospel. I said, I'm going to try something else. I'm going to try God this time.

"I picked up the Bible and started asking what to do so I could be a good Christian. Different preachers came to the jailhouse and they told me how to accept the holy spirit and how to be saved and all this stuff.

"I was sentenced to eight years in federal prison and I kept studying until I got out, which was about four years. I'd get up at five o'clock in the morning and go run a mile or two and then come right back and start reading scripture. I used to read scripture all day and night and then attend every Bible study course they had in the institution. I was sincere. I wanted to learn.

"The first persons I went to when I got back on the outside were Christians, because I didn't have anything and I thought they'd help me out until I got back on my feet. But it doesn't work that way—especially if you're coming out of prison. The people out there, the ones who call themselves Christians, they look at you as if you came to steal something from them. They don't believe you can be coming out of prison and be a Christian.

"I tried to show them what I had found in the scripture. I started teaching right from the book, not what Oral Roberts or any of the preachers

Pedro Martinez

Cut and Sew Room,
Prison Industries

thought, it was what was in the book. But people didn't want to hear that. Christians like having an abundant life and the scripture does not promise us an abundant life—at least not according to my studies. So I kind of blew their little bubble. They started rejecting me, pushing me out of church. In every church I attended, sooner or later the minister would say: 'Look, brother, I'm sorry, but if you don't change your way of teaching and your way of thinking you can't come to this church anymore.' The Christians pushed me out. I had to do something. So once again, I went back to drugs."

According to Rocky Shifflett, in addition to everything you can learn about crime by being in prison, close friendships among convicts can create strong ties and open new doors to opportunities in crime on the outside. It is not unlike the bond between former college classmates and fraternity brothers.

"I did six years on my first number," he said, fixing me with pale, serious eyes. "I went through Soledad, Tracy, San Quentin, those kind of places, and I met some heavy dudes. The result was I came out of the pen knowing how to do burglar alarms, paper games, all that shit. I had a list of international connections, people I could contact in other countries. All this because my word was good, because I was good. If I went to somebody and said I needed a front, that I could cover the bread in sixty days, I'd get it. I had made me good. But I had made me good in this society, I had become something in a society that wasn't the one I wanted to live in."

FIVE

The joint is a machine, but it's a human machine—I mean you've got humans at the controls. If it was a machine, we'd do our time and come out the other end, like things on a conveyor belt. But it don't happen that way. We do our time and if we offend a judge or a guard or somebody, those bastards find ways of keeping us in here, of punishing us. We pay for every little thing, including the right to get out. Complain and you're going to pay for it.

—Leroy G.

I was in Cell Block Two talking with Tomas Campos about doing time when the guard poked his head in the cell and announced it was time for morning count. If we wanted to continue, he said, I'd have to be locked in with Campos. His eyes said he did not recommend it. I told him to lock the door. It slammed and the key turned. "How long does this last?" I asked. Campos shrugged. "Could be a few minutes, could be two or three hours if they can't get the count."

The walls suddenly narrowed. The bunk with its wool army blanket and thin pillow was not much more than two feet wide. The table, supported by shelves, contained a few personal items—toiletries, snapshots, letters, cigarettes. The lidless steel toilet jutted out of the wall at an awkward angle, leaving only a narrow space between it and the bed. I had to struggle to keep from thinking of the cell as a coffin.

Time is the currency criminals use to "pay their debt to society." Convicts claim that this debt, calculated so months and years count for certain acts and deeds, is finally impossible to pay off—at least in the same way we pay off mortgages or loans. When the last payment is made on a loan, for example, the note is stamped *paid* and the matter forgotten. However, once a convict has paid his debt in prison, once he has finaled his parole, as a way of showing his desire to return to society, he still carries a brand. And perhaps that is the real punishment—both for the man or woman in prison and for the society.

One evening after I had spoken to a group of convicts in a federal prison in California, the imbalance between the sentence and the crime was made clear to me by Harlan Ferguson. "I'll be fifty-three years old when I get out and I will have spent almost thirty-five years of my life behind bars," he declared. "The sad thing is that if you took the money from every damn thing I ever stole in my whole life you couldn't buy yourself a new car."

"The simple fact is that you were sent here to do your time," said Steve Bishop. "Time is what they want out of you. And no matter how close you get to anyone in here, you're still doing this by yourself. There is almost no contact with your family. You're just about completely alienated from the outside. That's the worst part of it. I don't care if you're locked up with ten thousand men, you're still alone."

Some convicts welcome the idea of isolation. They feel a break is essential to bring about the adjustments necessary for survival. "I've never been able to do my time thinking about the streets or thinking about my kids or my mother—my loved ones," one woman explained. "I don't think I could keep my sanity or survive if I did. I love them too much, and I can't express that from here."

Robert Davis pointed out that certain temperaments are better suited to the rigid structure of prison life than others. Davis, considered dangerous even in the maximum security section of the pen, was put in cuffs for the interview. We talked at a table outside his cell.

"If you have a low threshold for coping," he said, "prison's going to be miserable for you. If you are a strong individual and have a strong character, chances are you'll fit in. If you're into the drug scene, then you'll do all right. If you are a loner and your character and physical strength are questionable, chances are you're going to have problems from the other inmates. But being locked up on a daily basis, mostly you adjust." He paused, then added flatly: "You adjust to the deprivation of your basic rights and the deprivation of your basic freedoms."

Basic freedoms are only the beginning. Juan B. noted that you also have to guard against being drawn into the prison machine, which is as treacherous as a whirlpool. "This pen gets rough, but that's a thing we have to live with. Sometimes there are racial problems, gang problems. You've got to keep away from all that, keep away from gambling, keep away from homosexuals, keep away from people who go out and sniff glue, keep away from the junkies. Because once you get involved in those things you usually find

yourself in some kind of a switch and you get PCed [put in protective custody] or somebody goes down."

In the Weight Yard, Folsom

Doing drugs is one way of doing time. But drugs create their own dangers. A high can take the edge off, push back the walls and free the mind from the clock; but drugs can leave you open to a bust or worse. As a convict in the prison hospital recovering from an overdose said, "Man, I can only take the loneliness so long before I need to get stoned and let it all drift away. This time, I happened to score some bad shit. It almost took me out. But maybe that's what I'm looking for."

Most of the people involved in the drug scene, like people I questioned about homosexuality and rape, either refused to talk about it or else denied its existence. But where money is involved there is always a way to get drugs—even for users shut away in a maximum security prison. Mexican heroin and cocaine seemed readily available. One convict said he'd heard that a guard, either working alone or as part of a group, brought drugs into

Glen Jaramillo (above)

Eugene Mescal (right)

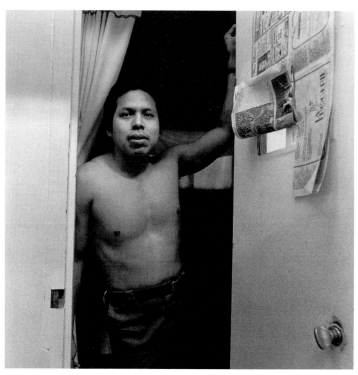

the North Facility, where they were distributed by members of a gang. Naturally, no one was mentioning names.

A young woman at the prison in Grants, New Mexico, said: "There's more drugs in this place than I'd ever imagined possible. I had never seen people shoot drugs into their arms until I got here. There's no way they can stop it. The girls here hide drugs in places guards don't think to look. They braid them into their hair. They put them into their bodies—in the place men don't have. They swallow a balloon with a bunch of bags of heroin in it and then vomit it up in the bathroom. They even exchange drugs mouth-to-mouth, in that single kiss you are allowed at the beginning of a visit."

Doing time, desperation gives way to cold resignation. "After a while," said Glen Jaramillo, a convict who was killed in a prison incident that occurred during the time I was working on this book, "you get so you don't want to feel nothing. You just do your time and try not to let all the things that were alive about you go dead."

Eugene Mescal remembered how he survived a serious emotional crisis with his sanity intact. "The worst day I ever spent in the penitentiary was when my brother died. He was always with me when I was growing up. So when he passed away in '85, I thought I was going to have to be admitted to the psychiatric ward. But I have one good friend here, Rudy Sena, and Rudy stood right beside me and said come on, man, you can do it. Those things are a part of life, you can't let this do you in like that. Be strong, start doing your time, don't let it get over on you. I thought a lot about the things he told me and I came through. I was depressed for a week, but I've seen some inmates either die inside or go to the psychiatric ward and totally become nothing."

Eugene unburdened himself of his brother's dying and his own experience of attending the funeral in chains by writing the following in the prison literary magazine:

It was 5:05 a.m. as I slowly walked out into the cold morning air to where the station wagon was parked. Carefully taking my steps not to trip over the chain between my ankles. Getting into the wagon with a small cage built in, and no door handles to pull on, nor handles to roll up and down the windows, wondering if they had built it just for me the day before. As we drove away from the penitentiary, I looked back at the prison. I could see the prison gun towers, fences, and the grey building with bars all around it. Lights at the prison shone like flares up into the sky. Man, was it good to get away for awhile, I thought, as we move down the highway at 75 m.p.h.

Stopped at Bernalillio to get on Highway 44 and drove in the early morning dawn. Stopped again at San Isidro to change drivers, and kept going down the road at 90 m.p.h., and around curves hitting 80 m.p.h. hoping that nothing would happen on the way to the funeral, putting my trust in God for a safe trip. Getting close to Cuba, memories came back, how I use to travel the roads with my brother, having a good time. After 4 hours we were in Farmington escorted to Brewer's Chapel.

As I walked in all chained up, I headed up the aisle toward the open casket. The church was filled with sounds of the organ as I made my way to the casket. There he was, laying so still and cold, as I put my hand on his forehead. I stood there looking. Seems like he was breathing, but yet he was dead. I had no sorrow or feelings, thinking, man, what has prison life done to me that I feel like a stone with no feelings at all.

"In here," Rocky Shifflett said, "I have to give myself goals that reach beyond tomorrow—because in a penitentiary you usually don't think beyond tomorrow. Because when you sit in one of those strip cells for ninety days, butt-ass naked in the dark, if you have a cigarette you have more than you've had.

"So they can't really take nothing away from you. I mean, what have I got to lose? I started with nothing, so anything I get is more than I had.

"I look at it like this," he continued. "How do you expect me to respect your system of justice when you will let a convicted rapist back out on the street before you'll let a junkie out? You want me to respect you, right? But I cannot respect you because even though I am a convict I still have morals and I have scruples. For me to live in a cell block with a man that's a child molester would be the same as condoning it. Society doesn't want him, that's why he's here. And I'm supposed to *live* with him? Jesus. I've got children. I can't condone it. I don't claim to be an angel. I commit crimes. I've committed a lot of crimes. I can't say I did it because I was a dope fiend. I knew what I was doing. But that doesn't mean I want to have to do my time with a bunch of rapists and child molesters. I guess that's what I mean when I say men start changing their goals and values in prison."

Rocky Shifflett

On Death Row, Eddie Lee Adams reflected about how he'd reduced his life to the few things he could do in a cell: "I write letters. I play a little music. All I've got to look forward to is today. I can't plan a week in advance. I can barely plan a few hours in advance—because I'm not in control of things. And me not being in control of them I have no say over them. And having no say I can't make them conform to my needs. And that is how Eddie Adams is spending the rest of his life."

He lifted his manacled hands and stretched the links between the cuffs. "The raw core of prison life, prison attitude, prison in general—it's something I don't wish on anybody. And if anybody's curious about what's happening in here, his curiosity is misplaced. I'm locked in this cell twenty-three hours a day. And the hour I get out to walk around ain't what's happening. It doesn't satisfy me. You know, this is how I'm going to be spending the rest of my life. And if somebody's interested in that then I'm willing to trade places, because I'm not happy. I'm not happy at all."

SIX

I see lots of women wearing pants when they come for a visit. Well, my old lady don't—she wears a dress. She looks real proper. Except she's got no panties or nothing under the dress. We work it so I can sneak my hand up there and stick my fingers in her pie. It's all that stiff pussy hair and juice! I go back to my cell smelling my fingers. I just lie on my bunk sniffing the sweet smell of her cunt on my skin.

—Anonymous

Love makes for hard time. During the years I have been involved with convicts, I've heard the stereotypical tales of the prison homosexuals, punks, and their enemies; I've also heard jokes about hemorrhoids and horror stories about gang rapes. They were all sensational and might have created the right tension to fuel movie scripts.

There were many more ordinary stories that dealt with the anguish of convicts with strong ties to lovers on the outside, real stories that said a lot more about the hardships of doing time. Convicts concerned about the problems that their being in prison caused their families. They worried that their children might follow their example. I was allowed to read the letters that broke off their relationships and to hear their stories of heartbreak, dejection, and attempted suicide. In prison, men and women watch their lives fall apart.

But there were happy stories too. I attended a wedding. I was taken into visiting rooms to meet a wife, a child, see a new baby. Some men claimed their love for the wife or girlfriend waiting on the outside was strong enough to sustain them. Some treated the subject with a romantic reverence. They created shrines from photographs; they wore the names of their lovers on their skin. Others, like Rocky Shifflett, whose sensitivity belies both his size and his reputation, found a vicarious release through poetry:

LAST NIGHT

last night i was again blessed
by the exquisite music that is you
delicate harmonies
still flowed from your body
the fragrance of flowers still followed you
i was for the first time since you left
  warm again
your lips kissed away the pain
of a thousand inquisitions

and then
with the coming of the dawn,
  you slipped away.

what was left of the night
slid down my questioning face
in a single teardrop . . . one
bird sang its terrible morning song.

The stuff of a whole lifetime could come and go in the space of a prison sentence. An Indian convict described how the relationship he'd formed on the outside during the time he was hiding from the police fell apart and how another grew in its place with a woman he met through a prison encounter group. That it continued to develop into a serious relationship seemed to leave him both bewildered and afraid but cautiously optimistic. "All I can do is hope it'll work out," he said and began his story.

"I'm here on a second degree murder that took place in the year 1979. I was plastered, and I'd smoked a little bit of weed with my sister and her boyfriend. We were all together on this particular cold night in the month of December. My sister's boyfriend slapped her—gave her a bloody nose. That upset me and I started to attack him. My sister jumped between us. 'No,' she said, 'you leave him alone. Get away from here.'

"I went out into the town and took it out on the first person that crossed my path. I split the town I was in and went back to the reservation and started living my life from there. I noticed a real change in myself. I was afraid to go out and get drunk again, so I just stayed home.

At a Convict's Wedding,
Main Facility, Santa Fe

*Body Builders, The Yard,
San Quentin*

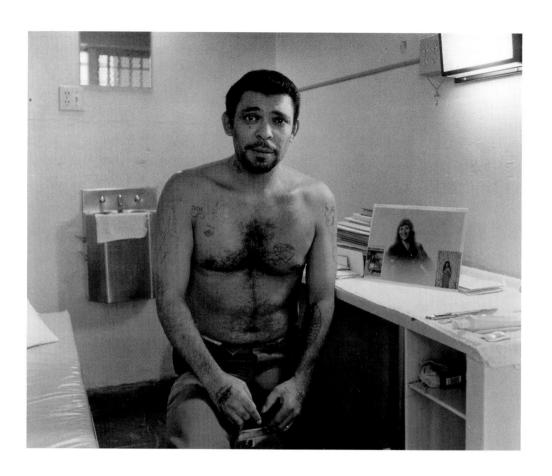

"I met a girl named Fanny Cowboy. She was a nice little girl and we lived together from 1980 to the time they found me and I got arrested in 1982. While I was at the county jail, she visited me often and wrote letters. Then when I came up here to the penitentiary she continued to come up with the children, but the visits were farther apart—once a month, then three months. One day she came up to visit and she told me that she had been seeing another man and that she wanted to be with him. I didn't get after her or anything. I just told her: if that's what you'd like to do go ahead. Just be careful of the things you do and take care of the children the best you can. With that, she left, and I have never seen or heard from her again.

"Six months later, I met a girl at one of these powwows the Indian Cultural people were sponsoring in the prison. We started corresponding. I'm a Navajo and she's a Pueblo but we seem to get along pretty good. She's been writing and visiting me often since then. Now and then when I get the chance I call her up.

"Things have just been going real good—that is, from where I'm at in here. Otherwise, I really don't know what she's really like. I just see her the two or three hours that we spend together in the prison. There's no contact at all—as much as we'd like to have it. We are only allowed one hug and one kiss at the beginning of our visits and then at the end. But of course when the guard isn't looking we get more than our share.

"I think things are going to work out with this girl. At first her family was negative. They kept telling her: he's a murderer and in a prison. He ain't no good. He's just going to use you. But after we sat down and talked, they started looking at me different. Now they are saying, if that's the kind of person you really want then the decision is up to you.

"Her decision was to continue the relationship. I know I'm going to be rejected by people out there. But I feel I am capable of handling it.

"I'll be getting out in six weeks and after all the time I've spent in this place I'm looking forward to it. Right now she's looking for a place for me to live and trying to find me a job, something to help me get a good start.

"I asked if I could come to live on the Laguna reservation where she is from but when she asked the authorities they said I couldn't be there because I was an ex-convict, a murderer. That made me feel angry, angry and upset at the entire Laguna tribe.

"There would be no problem for me to go back to my own people, the Navajo Nation. They would accept me and support me. I wish all other people could be that way. But they can't. I've got a jacket and people are going to be prejudiced against it. But I try to put those people aside and pretend that they don't exist, that they can't hurt me."

The Weight Room, Santa Fe

SEVEN

As I moved through the prison with my cameras, I became fascinated with the tattoos. I saw thousands of them. An astonishing number were done with great skill. They depicted everything from fantasy creatures engaged in combat with superhuman beings to orgies to Christ in all his moods. It was curious how often the face of Christ resembled the convict wearing the tattoo.

A few times, I encountered Justice. She was patterned after the traditional figure, blindfolded and holding her simple scales. I questioned a convict in the gym about his blind Justice, a statuesque figure draped so both full breasts fell free of her gown. "This is as far as it goes," he said, shifting a thirty-pound dumbbell from his right to his left hand and starting to count out a set of slow curls.

I asked what he meant.

"I mean, man," he grunted, "there *is* no fucking justice. The bitch's a whore."

I felt that the tattoos, under the guise of art, stood as signs of protest—conscious or not. They were part of a long tradition that had begun to flourish centuries ago in the prisons of France. Often the target was the system. Justice was a good example. After all, in the mouth of a convict, justice fails to have the same idealistic ring it has for the free man on the street. Again and again, convicts declared that justice and crime were parts of two separate systems and showed little kinship.

Sometimes the convict who spoke out seemed to understand justice,

The Virgin of Guadalupe
(above left and right)

Main Facility, Santa Fe
(left)

sometimes he didn't. From his own experiences, he could usually more easily describe what it wasn't than what it was. The bottom line was never simply innocence or guilt.

I remember particularly one convict's story. He had killed a man who had mistreated his sister and he felt he'd been sentenced too harshly by the judge who tried the case. He claimed the judge was insensitive to the passion that had caused him to kill the man. He did not dispute the guilty verdict. What he questioned was the punishment he had been handed.

"I was tried by an all white jury, white judge, white prosecutor and I had a white attorney defending me. It gave me no kind of a defense whatsoever. I was defended by a public defender, so they got paid by the same place—but from a different account. Therefore, I was lost at the beginning.

"The people that sentenced me didn't like me talking back to them. I told the judge I wouldn't change anything if I had to go all over again. I would do it just exactly the same. One of the prosecutors said I took off talking like a Fourth of July firecracker. His remark pissed me off so I told him off. That's my nature and if someone doesn't like it that's tough shit. Well, they didn't like it and they took it out in real harsh punishment.

"I had just got out of prison in Texas; I had just been out five and a half

Convict Outside the Gym,
San Quentin

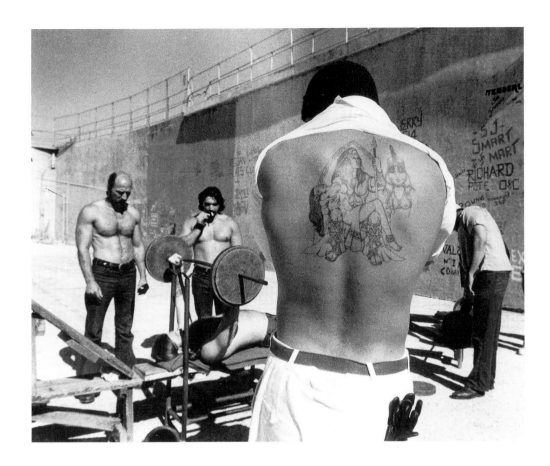

The Weight Yard, San Quentin

months. I did time on a twenty-five- and a twenty-year sentence and had been out five and a half months when I got into this. And then they gave me a straight forty-five years over here in New Mexico. I'm going to fight them all the way. I told them I don't believe in bowing down to any man on my knees. I'd rather die standing up on my feet and fighting than to bow down in defeat. And that's the part that these people dislike. To them, if I stand up and speak for my rights, I am a smart ass. They feel that a black man and a Hispanic man are supposed to humble themselves and say I'm sorry I won't do it again. Well, I will not say that to no man."

A second convict who did not question his guilt on the crimes he committed but who objected to the arbitrary way he was treated by the justice system was Phillip Cordova. He could already account for a lot of the rest of his life in his present sentence, but he said it might even have been worse.

"The judicial system in New Mexico is basically a railroad," he said. "I've been through the whole process twice, from the public defenders, DAs, courts, to this place. And once you're caught up in it, you're in a spot. Let's say you've committed armed robbery. Whether you've committed one or ten, they're going to book you on as many as they can in order to help cut down public pressure."

Main Facility, Santa Fe

We sat in the cafeteria. I had, from movies, come to expect the sound of metal soup spoons scraping against partitioned metal trays and creating a tinny cacophony that drowned out individual conversations. But plastics had done away with all that. Now there was only the annoying dry scraping of opaque white utensils against soft styrofoam trays and there was little of the old music in it. Behind us, a group of convicts began a noisy discussion and the young robber leaned over the table until his lips were within inches of my tape recorder.

"In my case, man, I was strung out. I was sitting in the courtroom, needing heroin, and there was this public defender I've known for all of about five minutes telling me what I would have to do. He had my life in his hands. The only thing I wanted to do was get back to the cell. I was sick. I needed some junk. They told me I could either make a deal and take twenty-nine years or not make a deal and end up with six hundred years. They said: 'If we have to put on a hearing it's going to cost the state and it's going to cost you.'

"I had to take what I got. And if I hadn't been strung out I might have took my time and fought it. I may have won and may have not. But at that time I just wanted to get to my cell and lay down. I sure didn't want no six hundred years."

EIGHT

I returned again and again to the New Mexico State Prison—even after I was certain I had finished shooting the photographs. I had been drawn into the lives of the convicts there just as I had at San Quentin, Folsom, and Lompoc. I found myself caught up in their dilemma, convinced it had an impact on the whole moral fabric of our society.

Visiting cell blocks, hospital units, kitchens, gyms, offices, and libraries, I kept trying to see a solution to a problem that few on the outside seemed eager to solve; and I wanted to be able to put it down in black and white, to have it show in the photographs, in the words. I wanted to create questions, to cause people to consider worthwhile alternatives that would effect some change.

I knew discussions were constantly in progress at the correction department and in the state legislature. But I knew, too, that the only answers being seriously presented were out of the middle ages—higher fences fitted with denser coils of razor wire, stronger walls with smaller windows, and, always, stricter security. Many prison officials considered such "improvements" the product of progressive thinking.

I had always sensed the danger in what I was doing. Weapons existed in the pen. Once, I saw a kitchen knife with a blade that had been given an edge and then sharpened to a point lying in the yard; it had probably been dropped by someone too frightened to carry out an ordered hit. Weapons

William Wayne Gilbert,
Death Row, Santa Fe

just like it, unsophisticated but deadly, were occasionally put to use and anyone inside could be a target. My own vulnerability was constantly in the back of my mind. The possibility existed that my presence might trigger a desperate act that would put me in jeopardy. A strategy had come to me unconsciously and repeated itself each time I felt the electricity build between me and an inmate or the members of a gang. Those times were not frequent, but they happened. It became a balancing act. In response, I scanned each situation quickly and learned to move immediately to the safest possible place. Though I am not argumentative by nature, I listened more than I spoke and rarely took issue to ideas that might lead to trouble. And I never allowed myself to be surrounded.

There came a day when I felt the twinges of those same fears even on the outside. It was July 4, 1987. I was driving home from a party when I heard a radio bulletin about seven convicts who had escaped from the North Facility. No more concrete information was given, but I put together fragments from two or three conversations I remembered from the previous few weeks and I knew immediately that William Wayne Gilbert, a convict I had first met on Death Row, would be among them. It was a chilling sensation that sent my mind searching for facts. The last time I had spoken to Gilbert he had said: "Something's going down. I can't talk about it right now."

Gilbert and I had struck up a friendship based partly on my interest in helping him publish his novel, *When Monkeys Cry*, a book about Vietnam. Reading it, I had been impressed by his knowledge of survival techniques and I now realized how helpful these might be on the outside.

As it turned out, Gilbert had masterminded the escape. Somehow he'd had a gun smuggled into maximum security, had wounded a guard, released a number of other convicts, and then fled with them through an opening in the roof. Governor Garrey Carruthers had issued a shoot-to-kill order.

I had ambivalent feelings about Gilbert. He was a convicted mass murderer who had, as I recalled, used post-Vietnam syndrome as part of his defense. While I didn't feel he would harm me, I also knew—if, for example, he was right about the post-Vietnam syndrome—that he could be unpredictable. He was a fugitive, a man on the run, under pressure and desperate to make good a chance that probably would never come his way again. What value was an untested friendship against those odds?

With each newscast, each report of no success, my uneasiness grew. I had loaded two rifles and two handguns and concealed them in my house. I was still convinced my family and I were safe, but I couldn't be sure. Finally, we left town. It was the first real rest I had had in weeks.

After a week, I returned to New Mexico. Some members of the escape party had been caught. Evidence seemed to indicate that Gilbert had fled the state and perhaps the country. But no one knew for certain. For days, nothing happened. The emphasis of the news shifted away from the fugitives, and gradually, life returned to normal. Then, one night during dinner, the phone rang. My wife answered. Her face went white. "It's for you," she said. "Wayne Gilbert—"

Wayne didn't talk long—I'm certain he figured my phone was tapped. He wanted to know about his novel. I had no news. He promised to be in touch.

From that moment on each time the phone rang struck new terror. There was no way of knowing where he'd called from—down the street or from another state—or where he'd be the next time.

The second call was almost a duplicate of the first. But it was shorter, as if he were under more pressure. I urged him to turn himself in. "I hear you," he said, and hung up.

Trial and error in this kind of relationship could be deadly. Even if I felt I could trust Gilbert, I didn't feel the same about the other two escaped convicts. The list of the three convicts' combined crimes ranged from breaking and entering to rape and murder. And they were desperate.

My wife, Dawn, and I talked about leaving again.

Then, a few days later, in an unspectacular raid on a California motel, Gilbert and the others were captured. A friend phoned to give me the news. I sighed with relief, but I was left with some very complicated feelings.

Now, remembering the episode of the prison break, I began to wonder if fear isn't a primary factor in almost everyone's dealings with convicts. Certainly, it influenced my experiences and kept me on edge. Now, weeks after my last visit, as I pause to examine a portrait, I sometimes feel I am seeing the prison in detail for the first time. I am still puzzled about the lack of color inside the pen. I saw everything as pure form—shapes, shadows, the chiaroscuro of black and white—and almost never as color. In the faces of some men I saw little evidence that being there caused them pain. Others had grown so accustomed to prison life that they called themselves "institutionalized" and confessed to actually being miserable when they were out on the street. But in the portraits of most people, I could see each day was a hell and its lessons were met with bitterness and hate. None of that would ever work to narrow the gap between them and the society that maintained the prison.

On my final day, I crossed the parking lot before I looked back at the prison buildings. Once again, they seemed to shrink down until I felt it was impossible that all I had seen and heard and felt could possibly have existed inside their walls.

Trustees, working in what appeared to be studied slow motion, paused and leaned on the handles of their tools to watch me put away my equipment. I got in and locked the door before I inserted the key in the ignition. The radio came on. I snapped it off, preferring to listen only to my own body.

I was still tense, still sweating. I relaxed in the seat and drove slowly along the tree-lined drive to the highway. On my left stood a gatehouse no

Convicts, Folsom

longer in use; its bulletproof windows were pocked from the impact of dozens of rounds of large calibre ammunition. I wondered who I could ask what had happened. Then I realized I did not want to know the answer.

I slowed once to pull myself together. Driving off onto the weed-grown shoulder and stopping the car, I looked back at the fenced buildings sprawled along the tops of the hills. This was the view most people preferred—if they wanted any view at all. The prison complex resembled an architect's model—unreal under the intense New Mexico sky.

I had friends in there. They were friends I'd made under special circumstances. I knew how easy it would be to regard them the way I had been taught I should—as convicts, dangerous people, possibly vicious, people not to be trusted—ever. But I knew that if I succumbed to those patterns, as I admittedly had during the escape, if I let that be the only viewpoint I was willing to accept, then I too would become part of the problem and everything I had learned, everything I had thought and felt, would never make any difference.

IN PRISON

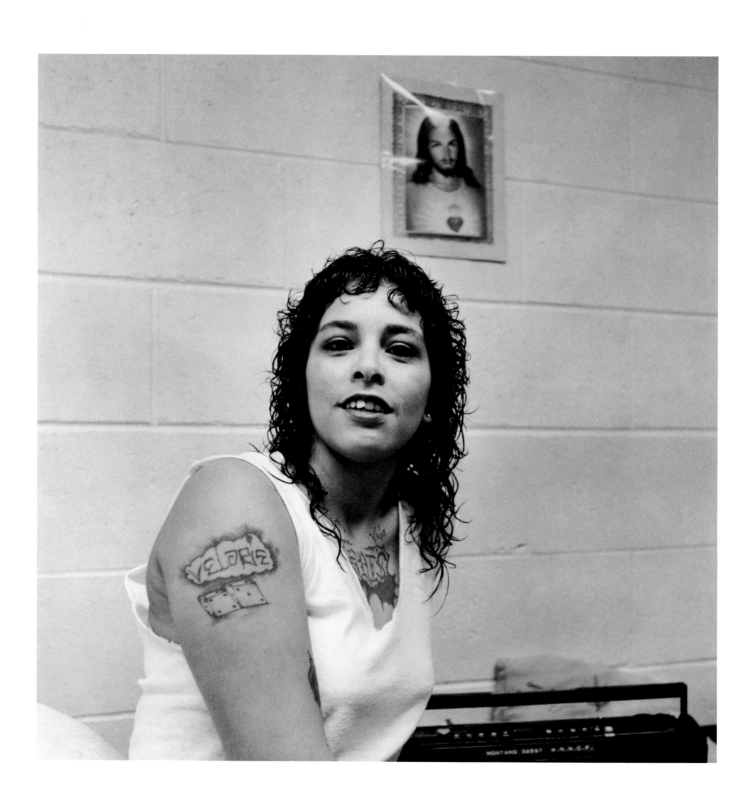

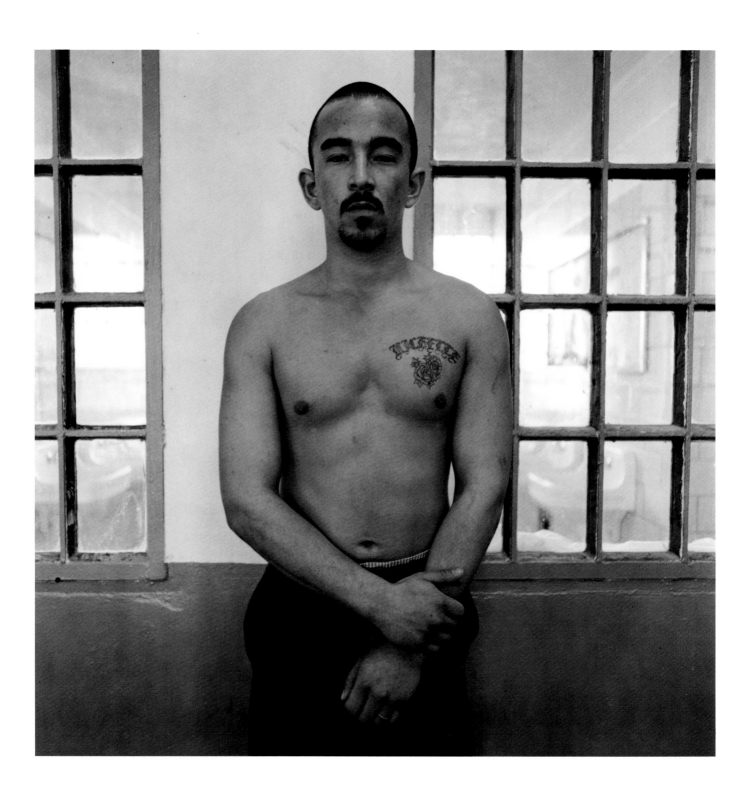